Be Deceived
No More
by
I Love You's

JOYCE NICHOLS

ISBN 979-8-89043-336-7 (paperback)
ISBN 979-8-89043-337-4 (digital)

Christian Faith Publishing
832 Park Avenue
Meadville, PA 16335
www.christianfaithpublishing.com

Printed in the United States of America

I do not believe it is by coincidence that any book you pick up when you want to improve yourself or just need some understanding or guidance is picked up by accident. I believe that although a person might not pray every day—I didn't—or be the ideal Christian and just happen to be in a bookstore and see a book that caught your eye was inspired for you at this moment. And what you have right now was meant to be.

This book intends to help you ease your pain in some way and hopefully guide you and help you get stronger in the Lord and understand Satan's romance scam of deception better. In fact, I prayed to God before putting this first word down that He guided my mind and writing of this book, and if only one person is helped, then I consider all this time and expense very well worth it. So please, take a deep breath, get comfy, let the knowledge be poured out, and be receptive to this information. All this in the name of Jesus. Amen.

Any biblical reference is taken from the New International Version (NIV) unless otherwise stated.

In the Beginning

To set the stage for the book, I will tell you a little about me. I was born and raised on a country farm. My parents taught me the meaning of life, hard work, and dedication to church and God. Other things include the importance of duties, values, character, integrity, tithing, being honest, never lying, and living in peace with your neighbor.

I am also a Libra person, so I have a very big heart. I don't know. Maybe that is the part God gave me—a big heart. I am often told by close friends and my girls that my heart is just too soft and so big, and I get taken advantage of by many people, and my heart gets stepped on easily. They say that I should not believe what everyone tells me to be the truth. Yes, that is biblical too—a wolf in sheep's clothing (Matthew 7:15), but inwardly they are ferocious wolves.

Little did I know that the trial and testamony of this book, made my weakness be tested. As what an athlete trains to be the best at his course, I was growing in strength with faith, love, and a desire for God like never before.

Through my trials, I have learned a great deal. I guess I would say the primary thing is to separate my soft heart from my mind. The Bible tells us so many things about the heart. That it is the most deceitful thing we have. Jeremiah 17:9 says,

> The heart is deceitful above all things and beyond cure.

The goodness of our heart determines our path. Proverbs 4:23 says,

> Above all else, guard your heart, for it is the wellspring of life.

Psalm 138 (the whole eight verses) talks about the attitude of the heart and how it will determine the action of our life. What you feed your heart, for example, listening to music, TV shows, your talk (confession) with friends, and your activities of daily living, will come out in your speech.

I have even noticed for myself that my old negative talk left me so much more depressed, and it came upon me so gradually. But once I changed things—listening to sermons on TV and Christian music, speaking to my cat and saying good things, changing my house around, lighting candles, thinking about God, and starting to memorize scripture—it gave me hope and life back to my soul. It worked! It was like my heart was pink again with life. That's how I felt.

Some may say that the zodiac signs are dealing with Satan and his tools when in actuality, the wise men were guided by the stars to find the savior in the manger. Matthew 2:1–23 talks about the wise men coming to worship the king. This is what is said in verse 2,

> Where is the one who has been born king of the Jews? We saw his star in the east and have come to worship him.

But I have had many people in my walk of life who are attracted to the calmness and fairness Libras exhibit. I do not allow *the spirits* to guide me because the Word also says that no one knows what tomorrow brings.

> Yet you do not know [the least thing] about what may happen tomorrow. (James 4:14b AMP)

Astrology is the study of stars to seek information about human events from the stars. Isaiah 47:12–15 talks about astrologers and stargazers who make predictions month by month, but there is not one who can save you.

Witchcraft displeases God:

I will set my face against the person who turns to mediums and spiritists. (Leviticus 20:6b)

Let no one practice omens, engages in witchcraft, casts spells, or who is a medium because anyone who does these things is detestable to the Lord. (Deuteronomy 18:10–12)

In Today's World

In today's society, the Internet and virtual, wireless communication systems can make me speechless because I don't understand the workings of it. I am not a tech kind of person, and I do not even want to understand how a person can talk to another that is halfway around the world in a matter of seconds. There are some gifted people who know the simple concept and just flow with it and use it to their advantage. Smile. I think this is also the age of the mind that can easily grasp this concept.

I can use apps and programs, and I am learning about Bitcoin (can't get my mind around that one fully) because I don't want to be ignorant of the progress the world is turning to. Now if you want to talk about what makes a good cookie or how a loaf of banana bread rises and can be so fluffy, or what makes a homemade chocolate pie set up, I can tell you the workings and whys of that pretty easily.

The worldwide information system is not always a good thing. Just like good people do bad things. Christians, or whatever title you want to put on yourself, is just that, a title. Only God knows the number of hairs we have. Matthew 10:30 says,

> And even the very hairs of your head are all numbered.

Only God knows the condition of our hearts.

> He knows the secrets of the heart. (Psalm 44:21b)

God knows the plans He has for us.

> For I know the plans I have for you, declares
> the Lord, and God also gave us free will to choose.
> (Jeremiah 29:11)

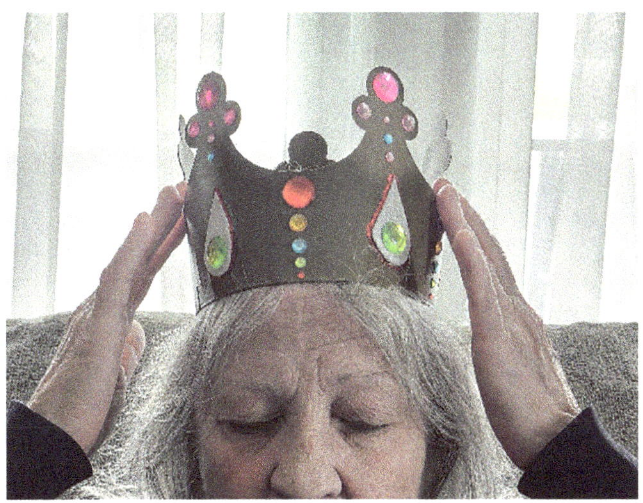

How Does the Enemy See Me?

So this book is about the scamming that is growing rampant all over the world—romance scamming. The dictionary defines *scamming* as a person who commits fraud or participates in a dishonest scheme. I was amazed at how the stores in my hometown are alerting consumers with warning signs at the cash register: "You can't get your money back once you send it," "Do you know who you are buying this for?" "If this is a scam, alert the police department immediately." Not only that, but cashiers are starting to question your purchase because they are aware of this *suspicious* activity, which is a large amount of money put on a gift card.

There are all kinds of deception in the world and even the Bible states that in the end-times, deception will be so much greater. Read 1 Timothy 4:1 and 2 Timothy 3:1–5, 4:3–4. The great deception is found in 2 Thessalonians 2:9–12. These verses talk about the terrible times in the end that will come.

Yes, I have been a victim of online scamming. I have lost money that I will never get back. It is gone. I was promised that they will pay me back. I was told many lies. In fact, I don't know what the truth is or what the lie is when I chatted with them. But I want to share what I have learned, and hopefully my story, my testimony, will get someone to believe this book from my experience and bless them and keep them safe.

I am not saying that online dating sites are bad or that they don't work. I know several people who have met their match and have gone further with their relationships or have parted ways. I have been on dating sites and have met several nice men. That is a key.

I met them in person. But you must also beware that even in person, not every person is real as who they say they are. Their talk will produce fruit in their actions and that is one way you will know a deceitful person. John 15 talks about Jesus being the vine, and we are the branches. Whatever we sow, we will reap in harvest, even in the contents of our talk. But know this too—reaping is not always instant. When planting a real seed in the ground, it takes a while for the seed to start with roots, with a stem, leaves, and then fruit.

There are a variety of ways but over 90 percent of the starting point is online in some way. Some of the apps and games I played were the door of opportunity that came toward me. It started as a simple friendly "Hello" or "Hey. How are you?" Just simple questions. I did not see there was harm in talking, so I did. I did not make it a point to talk every day or make scheduled time or even look the guy up or start the conversation. I say *guy* because my name is a good indicator that I'm a girl, Joyce. It's funny. I call him a guy, but it can easily be a woman who was conversing with me. So how does the enemy see me? An opportunity. They dangle what you want so badly—in exchange for your money. To separate you from the truth – from God.

I did not care if I missed any time with him. I did not care what he had to say. His opinion did not matter to me on anything, world events, or that I might be short with him. This is where Satan is patient. I had been talking to this person for a couple of months before I knew that I was looking forward to talking with him every day. I wanted to see what he was doing, how his night went, or what he planned for the day. It was beginning to feel like a real relationship. Before my prayer life changed, I woke in the morning, and my first thought was him. I got to get up and start talking with him. The talking is not a phone conversation, but typing on a chat site. Satan is patient indeed.

Chatting became an everyday routine, and I felt addicted to a special person. The flattery he gave me was softening my suspicious awareness of danger. I had blinders on. There is danger ahead and I was not aware of it. The conversation was changing subtly. It became more in the way of him saying, "I like you so very much," "I can't get enough of you." Then, out of the blue, it became deeper. Yes, he said those three words that everyone wants to hear—"I love you." Wow. I was thinking, *I don't really know you that well or you me, and although I'm a Libra whom everyone loves to be friends with, how can you say those three words and mean them? We have not met in person. Woah, slow down.* I'm reasoning this out in my mind and he doesn't know what those words really mean. He cannot possibly know what they mean. They cannot possibly mean them. It has only been a short time since we have been talking every day. *Red flag.* Yes, I saw it but chose to ignore it.

So I shrugged it off as he didn't really know what he was talking about. Really, he did not. I mean, I know I am an awesome person, but he didn't really mean what he said. *But what is the harm in just talking?* Those are my thoughts. He was making me feel good, and there was no harm, right? Do not ignore *red* flags, please. Let me say that again, *do not ignore red flags*, please. What do I mean by that? The gut feeling is that this person does not mean what he says, and if he does not mean what he says, then he is lying. Remember, believing a lie is a deception. Anything out of the ordinary that you raise your eyebrow to is a *red flag*. You must *not* ignore *red flags*. I believe we are all given a sense of awareness to alert us when something is not right and will harm us, when you cross the road, you look both ways so you won't get struck by a car. We are all given the Holy Spirit to guide us. It is our choice to listen or not.

For me, I started ignoring the "I love you" statements because they didn't mean anything to me, and he didn't really mean it. How could he? Now I'm wondering if I shouldn't have ignored my *red* flags or backed away from dedicating so much time with him. Yes, Satan has more patience than I do, and he is very cunning.

What is Satan's goal?

> The thief comes only to steal, kill and destroy. (John 10:10)

We must be vigilant and ever watchful, for the enemy is always prowling to see who he can devour. Something so innocent as talking to a stranger who makes you feel good doesn't seem like there would be any harm in the action. Right? That was my thinking.

Romance scammers target the lonely, no matter the gender. For someone to claim being of Christian faith is extra appealing to them. They think that Christians are supposed to be the *good kind* who always gives to the needy and have a soft heart for those who are in need. Remember, Satan knows the word of God as well. Satan is a deceiver, the master of all lies, wanting us to believe his lies.

> When he lies, he speaks his native language,
> for he is a liar and the father of lies. (John 8:44b)

Eventually, we will be so far from God that we realize his presence is no longer there like before.

> For Satan himself masquerades as an angel of light. It is not surprising, then, if his servants masquerade as servants of righteousness. Their end will be what their actions deserve. (2 Corinthians 11:14b–15)

Now we have our human side, the weak flesh, that is telling us that we need this every day, like a candy addiction. After all, the flesh is weak. Next comes little things that make us want more.

He was now telling me, "We need to meet." He said that he couldn't wait to look into my eyes and really tell me what he truly felt inside his heart for me. He said he never felt this way with anyone. "You are a dream come true. God sent you to me and my dreams are answered. Praise God." Yes, Satan uses God's name. He is not afraid to use Him as a means of getting what he wants. Satan knows what his fate will be in the end, and he is trying to get as many of God's creations to follow him into the pit of hell.

Scammers are evil. I say this because I do not see a good person that will actually lie to you straight in the face and can still be a good person. Is that even possible? This statement reminds me of this passage:

> With the tongue we praise our Lord and Father, and with it we curse men, who have been made in God's likeness. Out of the same mouth come praise and cursing. My brothers, this should not be. Can both fresh water and salt water flow from the same spring? My brothers, can a fig tree bear olives, or a grapevine bear figs? Neither can a salt spring produce fresh water. (James 3:9–12)

Well, that is straightforward and without question in my mind. But how do you know if they are scammers? Matthew 24:4 in the Amplified Bible says this,

> Jesus answered them, "Be careful that no one misleads you—deceiving you and leading you into error."

So if you pray from your heart and ask God to lead you from deception or reveal if a thing is deceptive, you must put your faith and trust in God that He will do just that and never forget the red flags. We cannot ignore those. But how long has it been that you spent time with God? When was the last time you felt his presence? When was the last time you opened up your Bible, and it wasn't on a Sunday? I am not here to cast judgment. I am merely stating how this happened to me. The questions I asked myself.

> If you hold to my teaching, you are really
> my disciples. Then you will know the truth, and
> the truth will set you free. (John 8:31–32)

Everything seems purely innocent in the beginning. Believing and knowing God intimately is your ace card, and not ignoring your gut feeling or questions you have in your mind is another indicator, but God gave us the Holy Spirit to guide us. It feels good to have someone that is a companion, someone who just wants to talk to you, someone who shows an interest in you. It all feels so very good. I personally know the feeling all too well. I have walked this road more than I should have, more than once, and it ends the same way—I've been taken advantage of and lied to. I reasoned in my head that I was a good person, and I'm online, and I can't be the only good person here. Right? I mean, maybe they are good people too.

Fear is not of God. I was busy with my life and loved being outside as much as possible. I was content because that is my happiness. I guess I did not realize that I was missing a man's sweet words, his attention, and the companionship that another person directed right at me. That fear of losing what I have not had in a long time made my mind lose all concepts of right and wrong. I think back on those times, and I am amazed at how I could easily give up money for this attention. The fear of being lonely was what I did not want in my life anymore. The fear of giving this up or losing it, the attention, and companionship kept loneliness away, and it felt so very good.

> Fear not; there is nothing to fear for I am
> with you; do not look around you in terror and
> be dismayed, for I am your God. I will strengthen
> and harden you to difficulties; yes, I will help

you; yes, I will hold you up and retain you with
My victorious right hand of rightness and justice.
(Isaiah 41:10 AMP).

Being out of daily reading in my Bible, daily prayer, and daily meditation had put me in this predicament. I had weakened my defensive wall. I had a crack in the door of my fortress that was around my heart.

But How do you Know?

1. Do their words line up with the word of God?
2. Their actions are a big indicator. Although you can't see them in person, their stories of past events and experiences can show you – listen to them without the 'fluff' and sweet words.
3. Trust your instincts – gut feeling, although subtle. That is where the Holy Spirit lives, inside of us. Don't ignore the red flags.
4. If you take out all those sweet words that warm your soul, what do you really hear?
   a. My sheep listen to my voice; I know them, and they follow me. John 10:27b

It's All About Money

The *I Love You* scammers only want your money, and with the unseen virtual world, they use this for their gain. That's what scamming is about you believing a lie. They are preying on people's good intentions. This is their job. They have a goal in mind. It is a challenge for them. They want to work hard to make their life easy. They want to set themselves up for an easy life at your expense. They do not have morals or the fear of God to face at the end of time. The job is not gender-related or even age-related. It does not matter what country you are from or the neighbor down the street or in the next town from you. They can be whomever they want to be—a successful businessman, a doctor, or a military person. There are no qualifications for the job. They can work in their slippers from home at all hours of the day or night. Their identity can be whomever they want to be. They can change gender and deceive many people at the same time. And scammers are getting very good at their job. All they need is a little crack in your time to open the door of opportunity for them to prosper. Does this sound familiar? Is this not what Satan does to attack you?

For me, I know what my weakness was, and yes, Satan came at me several times through that crack in the door. I was lonely at night, very lonely, and when a little bit of kindness and flattery was directed at me, I soaked it up. At first, it was a subtle *just-friends* type of conversation, but isn't that Satan's MO (mode of operation)? Satan is in no hurry to do his job. His first job is to get a toe in the open door of your life, your mind. And allowing him the time of day is his beginning success. For Satan knows what his goal is and is very confident he will succeed. Satan has time and is cunning.

His greatest tool he uses is deception. Deception is so great and everywhere today. More than I have ever remembered when growing up, or even ten years ago. Mark 4:19 says,

> But the worries of this life, the deceitfulness
> of wealth and the desires for other things come in
> and choke the word, making it unfruitful.

Being deceived is believing a lie. All this is predicted that more deceitfulness will happen closer to the end-times. This is just a form of deception that is growing so very fast—I love you. There are other very active deceptions—a deception as an emergency of your relative that you have to send money immediately, the everyday person on the street asking you for money when they are not really bad off, and your spouse telling you they worked late when they really didn't. Please, please take to heart what I am saying because it is getting stronger today than ever before. This is not only directed at women. I have heard stories of many men being treated this same way—deceived.

The First Deception—the Twist

Satan is bold as Christians should be equally bold. Satan knows the word of God and even used his twisted version of the word on Eve, the very first person to be deceived. Genesis 3 tells the story of how Satan came to Eve in the garden and was talking about the tree that was in the middle of the garden (verse 3). But when Satan questioned Eve about exactly what God said to her, that she will not surely die. Genesis 3:4–5 says,

> "You will not surely die," the serpent said to
> the woman. For God knows that when you eat of
> it your eyes will be opened, and you will be like
> God, knowing good and evil.

Satan was telling her that their eyes would be open and become like God with great wisdom, knowing all—to live in a higher state of existence than what they are presently living. She accepted the words of Satan that God did not mean what He said. She was deceived.

> The heart is deceitful above all things and
> beyond cure. Who can understand it? (Jeremiah
> 17:9)

> I, the LORD, search *and* examine the mind,
> I test the heart, To give to each man according to
> his ways, According to the results of his deeds.
> (Jeremiah 17:10 AMP)

That's not what God said. Genesis 2:17 says,

> But you must not eat from the tree of the
> knowledge of good and evil, for when you eat of
> it you will surely die.

Eve was deceived by the twisted word Satan presented to her. That same twist of words Satan still uses on us today.

Satan is bold enough to go to Jesus when He was in the desert and was tempted by him (Luke 4:1–12). Three times Jesus was tempted by Satan's twist on the Word of God. The Bible is so full of stories just like these. Although they were written a very long time ago, they are still meant for us today to learn from examples, and to guide us. Other famous stories on deceit are

1. Abram deceives Pharaoh in Genesis 12,
2. Jacob deceives Isaac in Genesis 27,
3. Rachel and Leah deceive their father in Genesis 29,
4. Potiphar's wife falsely accuses Joseph in Genesis 39,
5. The Midianites deceive Gideon in Judges 7,
6. Samson deceives Delilah in Judges 16:4–22,
7. Nathan exposes David's deception in 2 Samuel 12:1–15,
8. Job's friends deceive him in Job 4–42, and
9. Ananias and Sapphira deceive Peter in Acts 5:1–11.

Deception is a very serious matter, and it often leads to more sin, harmful repercussions, or destruction. We should try every day to be alert to the possible deception in others and ourselves. For ourselves, we must always strive for honesty in our words and actions in all areas of our lives. For when we lie, we sin against God—not just to ourselves and other people.

> The Lord detests lying lips, but he delights
> in people who are trustworthy. (Proverbs 12:22)

The Bible is our daily reference for living the good life. Maybe we should use Jesus's example and use those exact words and memorize them in our hearts to fight back, which is what God told us to do.

I have hidden your word in my heart that I
might not sin against you. (Psalm 119:11)

By knowing the Word of God and saying "It is written," Satan no longer has the power to use his weapons against us.

Satan is defeated by the words we use. We have power over Satan. *You* have the power over Satan. *You* can shut him down. If you believe in your heart without a doubt that Christ is the son of the living God, *You* can shut him down. Even speaking the name of Jesus, God, and the Holy Spirit will have Satan shaking in fear. We have power over the enemy. Luke 10:19 says,

I have given you authority to trample on
snakes and scorpions and to overcome all the
power of the enemy; nothing will harm you.

Believe in the word. Get into the Word of God and believe who you are. We have the same power through the Holy Spirit over Satan. We just have to use that power, and our greatest teacher is Jesus. *You* can do this.

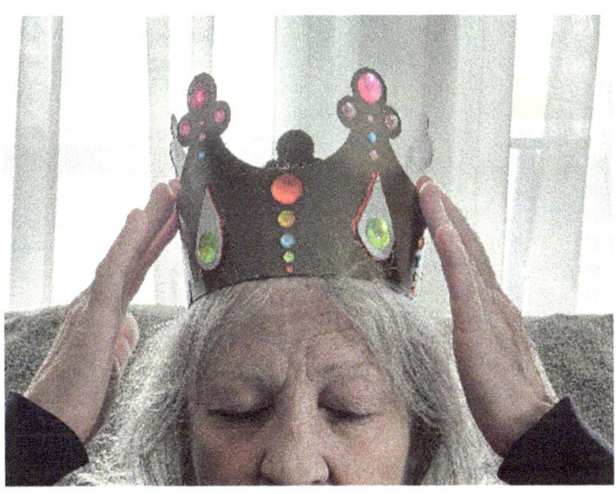

My Anger

I will be honest, I got mad—very mad—that Satan was attacking me. But I also know that the good that came out of his attacks made me a better and closer Christian toward God. James 1:2–4 says,

> Consider it pure joy, my brothers, whenever you face trials of many kinds, because you know that the testing of your faith develops perseverance. Perseverance must finish its work so that you may be mature and complete, not lacking anything.

2 Timothy 3:16–17 says,

> All scripture is God-breathed and is useful for teaching, rebuking, correcting and training in righteousness, so that the man of God may be thoroughly equipped for every good work.

Romans 8:28 says,

> And we know that in all things God works for the good of those who love him, who have been called according to his purpose.

But think about this. Satan's goal is to attack and discourage and trip us up and get us to doubt and to be defeated and *not* believe in God and His Word. So I ask myself, how can I be mad at that? Smile.

A wise woman once told me this true statement: "The storm doesn't stay in one place for very long, and then it moves on." This is the same concept. If Satan knows that his attacks are not doing anything to you, and he hears and sees the strong conviction you are showing, he knows he is defeated. But that does not stop him from attacking you from a different side or angle. But do not be discouraged. You are growing stronger every day by changing and fighting. It is like a baby learning to stand. You may be wobbly at first, but the more you do it and the more you practice, the more your determination shows and the stronger your muscles get, and the wobble goes away, and then you start standing. Before you know it, your head is held high—that you made it through the storm. *Yay*!

I know I am not the only lonely person who lives alone, is retired, and is faced with this same kind of problem; and if you are that person I just described, then I am here to help you get out—or avoid—the pit.

The Bible talks about loneliness and what Moses, Solomon, and many others went through. It says that our loneliness is temporary and also a season of learning. If we don't go through trials, how can our faith be increased? Why would we need to trust Him if life is easy and we don't need God?

The word also tells us that we are never alone although we may feel it.

"God has said, 'Never will I leave you; never will I forsake you.'" Hebrews 13:5b

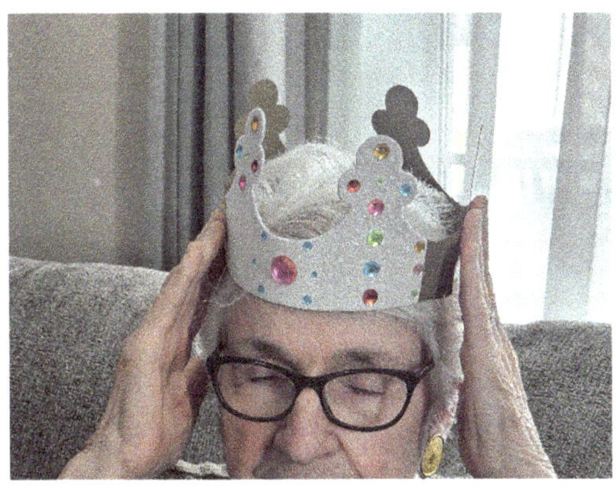

My New Routine

Every morning when I first wake up, I am on my knees praying to God. Being on my knees is how I pray and show honor to God Almighty. I have this desire to be with Him. I cannot wait to be with my Lord, and this desire has been growing inside me ever since I started and stayed with this routine. This is *our* time, just between me and God. I cannot wait to start telling Him things. There have been times that I do not know what to say, so I say the Lord's prayer. There have been times that I seek specific things and the more I do my morning prayer every day, the more I want to do it. It is my desire that is growing and wanting more, and almost every time I pray, I cry. I can count on my fingers how many times I haven't cried. And I do not care. It does not matter what my face looks like. What matters is that I spend time with my Lord, and He sees the desires and condition of my heart. All I know is that I am putting God first in my life, and it has given me peace and reassurance that I am going to make it. That I am *not* alone.

I also pray that God guides and directs my path for that day. I know without a doubt that God can stop me from doing anything because He has done that. But look at God this way: Would your earthly father deny you anything you ask of him? Then would God deny you what you ask of Him? Remember, we have our own free will, and we can choose to do what we want while on this earth. *But* we don't always get what we want or receive right away. This reminds me of the country song "Unanswered Prayers." God does know what is good for us, whether to answer a prayer now or down the road, or not at all.

As a mother who raised five children, it gives me great satisfaction knowing that my grown children want to spend time with me without encouragement from me or inviting myself over. Well, that is what God wants too, for us to willingly come to Him not only in the morning prayer time but also throughout the day. And that is what I do as well. I may be sewing and feel a tug at my heart and get up and leave the room to be with my Lord. I sometimes look out the window and am amazed at the beauty I see. God gave me this day as a present, and I want to thank Him for it. I say things to Him like I would a friend. Can you imagine how that makes Him feel? Can you imagine God smiling at you because you took the time to be with Him? James 1:17a says,

> Every good and perfect gift is from above, coming down from the Father of the heavenly lights.

All good things!

Devotions, Meditation, Bible Times

I have a devotional book that I read after my prayers, and I jot down my feelings and what I have been thinking, and what the devotion meant to me. Lately, my prayer has been answered in my devotion. And I just think it is so amazing that God has a hand in it. I mean, I am nobody special except to my kids, grandkids, and a few close friends. But that's not how God sees me. I am very special, and He will put in our path what we need and our answers to our requested prayers.

Every one of us is very special. Every one of us. You who are reading these words: *You are special* to God. *You* matter to Him. *He* came to die for *you*. *He loves you*! You have made mistakes in your life, but the love He has for you is so immense and deep that He still urges you to come to Him. He is not mad at you. He *loves* you. God cares for every detail of my life—of your life.

I found a picture of a woman wearing a crown, and the words said this: "No matter how people treat you, never forget…*you are a daughter of the king*!" Smile. That is in my Bible now to remind me I am a daughter of the king. I am a joint heir with Jesus Christ. Romans 8:17 says,

> Now if we are children, then we are heirs—
> heirs of God and co-heirs with Christ, if indeed
> we share in his sufferings in order that we may
> also share in his glory.

I also spend time reading the Word of God. Because everything I need to know, every question I need answered is there. John 8:31b–32 says,

> If you hold to my teaching, you are really my disciples. Then you will know the truth, and the truth will set you free.

Meditate on the word. Chew it up in your soul. Write it on your heart.

> Do not let this Book of the Law depart from your mouth; meditate on it day and night, so that you may be careful to do everything written in it. (Joshua 1:8)

> But his delight is in the law of the Lord, and on his law he meditates day and night. (Psalm 1:2)

> I have hidden your word in my heart that I might not in against you. (Psalm 119:11)

Please! Please! Help Me!

After a time, the conversation changed to an unexpected twist in his situation, the financial situation. He asked for a small amount of money with a promise that he would repay me back as soon as possible. I was told that his account was locked up, or he was out of the country on business and couldn't get to his money. Just as soon as he would get back, he promised to pay me back. He even swore to God that he'd pay me back.

James 5:12 says,

> Above all, my brothers, do not swear—not
> by heaven or by earth or by anything else. Let
> your Yes be yes, and your No, no, or you will be
> condemned.

"Okay, mister, where is my proof that you are real?" He'd send me a picture of himself. Remember, we are in the cyber world now, and the Internet is full of pictures everywhere. The Internet can be used for our purposes too, but you cannot believe everything on the Internet. I have looked up names in certain states and sometimes cities. I have looked up my own name under the white pages to see what I can find information about me, and it is amazing what I found. This is their job in the comfort of their own home, in slippers.

We now get to another step, which I just cannot handle personally. I do not like to be pushed. When the money was brought up in conversation, it was an immediate response that was needed right away. Immediately! Like today. "Go, go fast, and do it today." He'd die if I didn't do something today. His very life depended on my help. I didn't want to be the cause of his death, do you? He'd give me direct and specific instructions equipped with name and address on where to send the money. Cash was always best, of course. Even the government cannot track cash. Now I didn't have proof that I sent money, just a name and address, and the receiving end never received anything. Yep, I have heard it all. I have been there. Please listen to what I am saying to you. Please.

Technology is getting even trickier because of cyber money, cryptocurrency, and digital currency. I mentioned Bitcoin earlier. *Cryptocurrency* is defined as a medium of exchange through a computer network. This eliminates the need for banks, and the funds are sent from one source to another electronically. Cryptocurrencies are not currencies like what I grew up knowing as money. It is not a physical form like money and is not issued by the government. The definition of crypto is a type of digital currency in which a record of transactions is maintained and generated by the computational solution of mathematical problems. This is not government controlled or insured like in FDIC, which most institutions are backed with, giving you peace of mind. At first, it was very hard for me to understand the concept. Although I have used cryptocurrency, it still cannot be withdrawn or cancelled once it is sent out.

The strong point I want to make is that from the beginning of the first *red* flag, know that 99 percent is not real, not real words, not real feelings, and most likely not the real person who you think is true. I also wrestled with this *real-person* issue. After all, I'm a real person, honest and good and God-fearing woman, and surely there are real men who are the same as me, right? That was what I was wrestling with, and I did not want to question God, but I had tunnel vision because I was so very lonely. And here was a guy who was stroking my needs and making me feel good with flattery and I'm needed. But Satan is the father of lies.

John 8:44 says,

> You belong to your father, the devil, and you want to carry out your father's desire. He was a murderer from the beginning, not holding to the truth, for there is no truth in him. When he lies, he speaks his native language, for he is a liar and the father of lies.

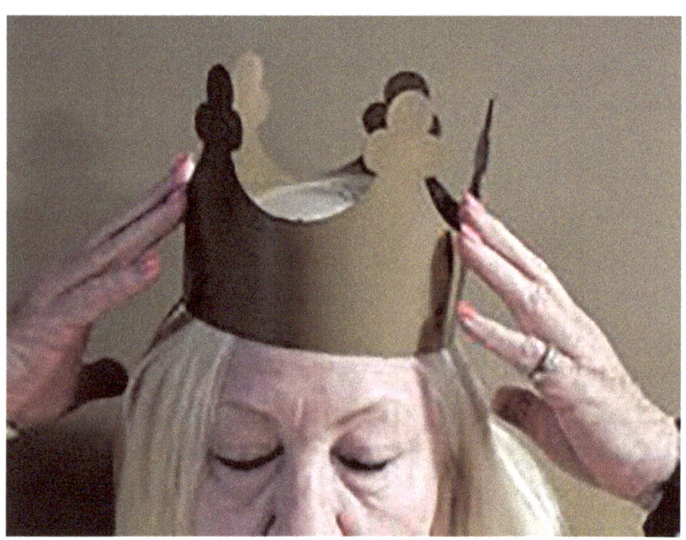

Gifts

There were times that I received in the mail a sign of endearment which was a stuffed teddy bear. Now, I'm a grandma to beautiful grandchildren, and I guess I feel I'm too old to receive a child's gift, but it was done to me, twice. My first reaction was, "Aaawwwww, how sweet." I felt that was just another attachment to my heart. Then I was thinking, *He* must *be real.* It was another string to pull me back in and keep me under bondage to him (or maybe a *her*?).

Now, I was feeling stronger and hopefully wiser in this *relationship*. After several months, or however long it had been, I started to ask questions. "Hey, mister, what is your home address?"

He answered, "Why?"

"Because I sent you mine, and I want yours now."

You could tell he was dragging his feet about answering me or ignoring the question, but eventually, he may give it up. I looked up the address, and it was an empty house that was on the market to be sold or had been sold. I was scratching my head and asking, "Hey, what's going on? You never told me this. You could get your money here instead of asking me to send you my money." Here we go, another excuse. Another lie. That was if he answered my questions at all. So now, I had a fake address with no proof it really was his address.

Another thing that happened to me was this. I got a chat request from him that said, "Surprise. I'm in a hotel close to you!"

"What? Are you serious? Now I get to see you in person and look into your eyes and touch your skin, and we can finally talk like a real couple. Okay, where are you so I can come and see you?"

Then he would tell me I must pay him first because it was very important that he would get this debt paid immediately, like right this very minute.

"Hurry. Go and do it right now. Hurry, hurry, and I cannot wait to see you, my darling." I do as he asked because I couldn't wait to see him. It was very important to me that I see him. All my doubts would wash away and be there no more. I would get to see him in person.

I told him I sent the money and show him proof of the receipt that the money was sent—it was *cash*. Overnight. He told me that I needed to go get some gift cards, the maximum amount, and send them to him, and then he'd tell me where he was staying.

I was thinking, *Are you kidding me?* I have to pay to see you? But because of the type of person I am, I did just that so I can see him because I need confirmation or closure. He told me that one of the gift cards didn't work, and I had to go get one more. Okay, I have a high tolerance for pain, and I am a really naive person but eventually, I wised up, and I said, "No, I am not going to do it. Everything has been going your way, the way you want it, no questions asked. Not anymore, mister. No."

Now here came the really hard part for me. When I pushed him away, he gave me his very best tongue-lashing. He literally said all kinds of mean and hateful things to me that I know were not the truth. People have to pretend I'm bad so they don't feel guilty about the things they did to me. Read that again because it is so true. They know they are fake and did wrong. Also, a defensive response is a sign that Satan has deceived you.

And the Word of God says this about the tongue.

> The tongue has the power of life and death,
> and those who love it will eat its fruit. (Proverbs
> 18:21)

Now I was blamed for making him mad and saying mean things to me. It was now my fault for all that happened. I was at fault for being disrespectful to him and how dare I talk to him that way. How could I say I was a Christian by refusing him his needs and not making things run smoothly? Lies. They were all lies, and I was not expecting the tongue to slice my heart, and it happened anyway.

Let's Do a Trial

I did a trial when I was pressed to send more money because I felt that I had invested so much already. I really wanted my money back. Let me remind you that Satan does not give up just because you might have won the battle. If I am saying I am a princess, and my Father is the number one Father whom I live for, God. I am going to act like it.

I told my guy the scammer that my father refused to talk to me about him. This was true. I cannot get God to talk to me about him at all—not one word. I was not going to lie. I was not going to stoop to the devil's level and lie. I told the truth. I felt as though I could not get God to answer me. God did not talk to me about my guy. I have begged and pleaded for God to tell me something, anything, and nothing came from God. So in telling my guy that my father loved me so very much, God the Father does love me very much—truth. My inside was saying no more. And my guy backed off. I was no longer pressured. I feel as though I have won another battle. Woohoo! Do you see what just happened? I spoke the truth to what I know and believe in my heart to be real and honest and good.

So the scammer came to me in a different way to ask for money. He wanted me to send him money for a plane ticket, and he would be on his way to me. He promised that he'd do the plane ticket. Then the begging came, the pleading, the disgrace he went through just to do that, beg. But he did it anyway. But did he come? No. I offered to make the reservations for him—absolutely *not*. He would *not* stoop to have a woman take care of him that way. He was fully capable of doing his own travel arrangements. So after I sent the money to see him, he did not send the itinerary to me because an emergency came up, and he had to use the money for other things instead of a plane ticket. I was just shaking my head. How naive was I? How stupid was I? How could I believe him? The definition of *naive* means showing a lack of experience, wisdom, or judgment. I would say that's me—this Libra person who wrote this book.

I reminded him that he promised me this or that. But he ignored my statements like I never wrote them down. He did not respond to them. When I pressed harder for him to answer me, he started to get irritated, and more accusations were thrown at me. Some of the verbal abuse I got from the scammers were very hurtful to my soft heart. Literally, I have been brought down to tears because of the verbal abuse.

When I insisted that he start paying me back because I needed my money to pay some bills, he stopped chatting with me. Now I could not get him to talk to me at all. He was gone. When I started using the words he spoke to me, he had nothing to say now. It was like he dropped off the face of the earth, nowhere to be found. Please, please, listen to what I am saying.

Satan's goal is to weaken our faith—to question what we know to be the truth. Once this is done, he doesn't have to do anything else. Ignoring the wisdom in God's word; not applying it to our life; and not reading, meditating, and spending time with God, we lose wisdom of knowing what is right from wrong. Proverbs 1:7 reads, "The fear of the Lord is the beginning of knowledge, but fools despise wisdom and discipline."

But I learned this. To really know God, I have to spend time with him like what I do with my girlfriends. I know that one gets depressed on certain days. Another has the same desires that I have—what their likes are and what will set them off, their goals for the future, and what they endured in their past that makes them how they are today.

How do I know this? Because I spend time with them, and we talk. Time is a key. Anything you feed always gets stronger than what you ignore.

Satan tells us, "If it feels good, it must be right. It must be okay to do it if everyone is doing it. What harm is it to try it at least once?" Is a light bulb coming on in you?

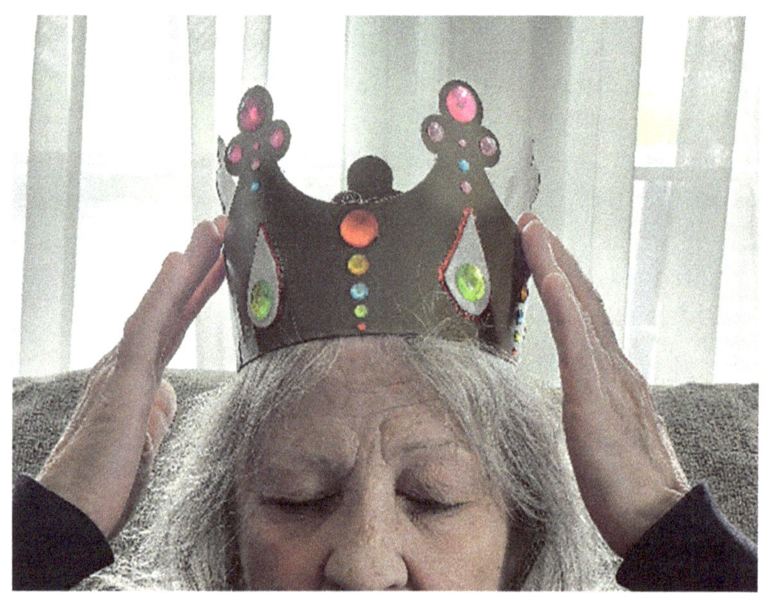

What I Learned

But what I have learned from all this I want to pass on to you, and please don't forget this. God sent us the Holy Spirit to be our comforter. When I felt my heart was bruised, hurt, and bleeding, I asked the Holy Spirit to come and put salve on my broken heart and to heal it and not make it hurt so bad—and it worked.

> He heals the brokenhearted and binds up
> their wounds. (Psalm 147:3)

> The Lord is close to the brokenhearted and
> saves those who are crushed in spirit. (Psalm 34:18)

I am the one who makes my choices in life, my decisions. I choose to hunger for God, for he loves me so much. I choose not to use my emotions to make decisions anymore because when I do, I am sinning. I will mimic Jesus when he walked the earth and be stable in the storms I go through. I will pick myself up and face life head-on. I will! I will! I'm not saying it will be easy or that I won't make mistakes, but I will strive to be better and learn from my mistakes. I will!

Sure, I cried some, and I knew they were lies but I also know that I am a child of God. I love God with all my heart, and I am a princess, a joint heir with Christ. Now I would straighten my crown, straighten my back straight, and act like who I am, a princess.

This was what I did to set myself up for success in my very being, my soul. I found sayings and verses that remind me of who I am. I have them in my Bible, in my bedroom, and anywhere that

I spend a lot of time. I was reminded of who I am. I am a child of God, and my Father would take care of me. I used scripture and told God that His Word says this and that. I memorized scripture that I say during prayer time.

> For we know that in all things God works for the good of those that love Him, who have been called according to His purpose. (Romans 8:28)

The most difficult experience we go through, God can turn it around for our good. I have seen it work. I have experienced this firsthand. I still say this scripture whenever I am in a difficult time. I remind my father what is said, and it helps me. God does not need reminding of His words, memorizing is for my benefit.

I had to lose what I felt was everything so God could show me who I was. He did not want me to put my trust in material things and money. I found myself. I am a better person. My relationship with God is stronger. He woke up the lion in me. I am a soldier. God is about to restore everything I lost. I didn't do anything wrong. I feel that in my loss, I am looking, searching, yearning for, healing and trusting in Him more. I can see the smile on God's face by that confession.

> I have hidden your word in my heart that I might not sin against you. (Psalm 119:11)

If we have the Word of God in our heart and memorize, repeat it, and say it out loud, then we are better equipped when adversity comes to us.

Look at this, if Satan is hearing you say the scripture, why would he want to stay around you? He is fearful of the powerful word of God. There is power in God's word. Hebrews 4:12–13 says,

> For the word of God is living and active. Sharper than any double-edged sword, it penetrates even to dividing soul and spirit, joints and

marrow, it judges the thoughts and attitudes of
the heart. Nothing in all creation is hidden from
God's sight. Everything is uncovered and laid
bare before the eyes of him to whom we must
give account.

You can take this to the bank and know for certain it is true and
powerful.

Here is another thing that is important to know. God will use
this hard time. I am leaning into Him for comfort, and He takes the
broken pieces and makes something beautiful. God is a jealous god
for you and me. But I have learned and I know that God will use
the evil things of this world and turn that around for our good. God
is there most definitely, without a doubt, but from my own experiences, I want you to learn and know that not all is lost.

Peter explains trials, refining fire and impurities this way in 1
Peter 1:7. The trial of your faith increases as it's exercised. The trials
come so your faith—of greater worth than gold, which perishes even
though refined by fire—may be proved genuine and may result in
praise, glory, and honor when Jesus Christ is revealed. This fire will
get rid of impurities. When gold is heated to the melting point, the
impurities are separated from the true gold. Faith is refined in the
middle of trials. Trials are hard and hurt. They have sacrifice, suffer-
ing, tears, and pain; but they bring strength to your faith. It produces
a good thing if you will let it.

For it is God's will that by doing good you
should silence the ignorant talk of foolish men.
(1 Peter 2:15)

I see that my risk, loss of money, my time, and tears were for a
dream no one can see but me. Am I sorry? No, because I know that
my soul, my very being is closer to God. I memorize His Word and
know that God will use the evil things of this world and turn that
around for my good. This trial has put me in a fire of testing, and I
will be victorious in the end and give God all the glory for it.

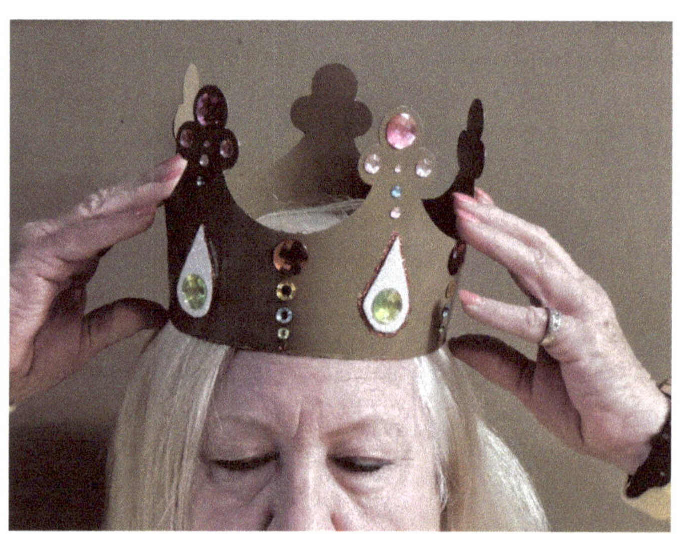

The End

The end is here—your savings was gone, and you were in debt. I heard that some women even had to mortgage their houses. They had to move in with their kids to survive, and the mystery man was nowhere to be found. The man who said that you owned his heart is—*poof*—gone. Yes, this has not happened to only me. There are so many women who have been and are scammed, even today. In fact, there are many, many men who are scammed as well.

My children help me with my loneliness at every opportunity, and I am so grateful for them. Although they don't fully understand my circumstances or feelings, they are my support, and they are there. The feelings I had while going through this was a huge embarrassment because I believed in someone without reserve. But that is who I am. That doesn't mean that the other silent victims are without the same feelings and will carry this secret to their grave. So the exact number of people who have been scammed by *I love you* will never be known. I do not want to confess this to anyone. Anyone. *But* enough is enough, and I want to help someone so desperately. I don't want anyone to feel this pain I have felt.

As I said earlier, my parents raised me as a hard worker and told me to take the tongue beatings from others in silence and go on, that God will take care of it all, that I need to get up and dust myself off and go on with life. And that is what I am doing now. I keep my mouth shut about all this. I cry in my home alone, by myself. I talk to God so freely. In my prayers, I have repented from believing a lie and not seeking out God's Word first. I wipe my tears, learn from this, and go on with life. I am rebuilding my savings account. I look at myself as a princess, adjust my crown, stand up tall, and hide under God's protective shadow. Psalm 91 is very good to read over and over, to hide under God's protective wing.

I hang onto every word in the Bible, learn scripture, write it down, keep it close to my heart, and let the healing begin. I listen to sermons on TV. I quote scriptures out loud. I memorize verses. I sometimes cry and then sing songs. I am working hard to get Satan's lies out of my head. I do not want to hear his whispers. I do not want to be reminded of how it felt to chat with someone who really wanted to chat with me. I do not want to miss the "darling," "sweetheart," and "I love you." I want more of God. I want more of the Spirit, and I am getting the desires of my heart because that's what I'm pursuing. Here are some of the scriptures that have helped comfort me:

> For God will bring every deed into judgment, including every hidden thing, whether it is good or evil. (Ecclesiastes 12:14)

> Do not be deceived: God cannot be mocked. A man reaps what he sows. (Galatians 6:7)

> He heals the brokenhearted and binds up their wounds. (Psalm 147:3)

> The Lord is close to the brokenhearted and saves those who are crushed in spirit. (Psalm 34:18)

> Yet if he is caught, he must pay sevenfold, though it costs him all the wealth of his house. (Proverbs 6:31)

> Do not steal. Do not lie. Do not deceive one another. (Leviticus 19:11)

Your attitude should be the same as that of Christ. (Philippians 2:5)

But I tell you; love your enemies and pray for those who persecute you. (*This* was hard for me to really do from the sincerity of my heart) From the sermon on the mount we are instructed to love our enemies and pray for those who persecute us, that we may be children of our father in heaven. (Matthew 5:44)

The Lord is known by his justice; the wicked are ensnared by the work of their hands. (Psalm 9:16)

Lying lips are an abomination to the Lord, but those who act faithfully are his delight. (Proverbs 12:22)

He shall call upon Me, and I will answer him; I will be with him in trouble, I will deliver him and honor him. (Psalm 91:15 AMP)

Although I don't want harm to come to this person because that's not what Christ would want, I just want what was promised to me. There are so, so many verses that I could put down here, but those are the ones I cling to for comfort. Not only the Lord and the Bible reading but also the prayers I said, the devotions, the comfort from other Christian women, and writing this book have helped me so much. I want to share my testimony so that at least one person will be helped and avoid what happened to me.

So I look back and think about this and the times before. How can I ever know if this is a real thing or fake? Well, the Bible says in Matthew 7:15–20 that we will know them by their fruits. What is in their heart should be evident and demonstrated in their talk because we don't see them in person and most likely do not talk to them on the phone. Some things seemed to contradict what he had said earlier, but I either chose to ignore that, reasoned it out, or thought that it was my mistake and that I understood things wrong—a red flag I ignored.

So this is what I have come away with for my learning. I am most definitely not going to spend time chatting with anyone online. That is just a crack for the devil to get into my life and mind. For me, I have such a very soft heart that I want to help anyone in need. If I avoid online chats, then I will come out better. My God knows all my wants, desires, and needs. Staying so very close to Him will give me all the comfort I need for the day. Today is the present, and we are told to live in the day we have and not worry about the future or tomorrow.

But if you find yourself starting, or in the middle of the same situation I have talked about, know this without a doubt, I do not have anything to gain in telling my story. You have lots to gain by taking time out of your day to read this. No matter who he says he is or what he will/or has promised you, you have a choice. You can continue with him, and in the end be without him, his sweet words, and your money. Or you can stop chatting with him right now, heal, and know that you will be okay. *You* are a princess. *You* straighten your crown up, stand straight, and know inside who you really are.

You are responsible for the condition of your heart, only you. You may have tears running down your cheeks while standing there, but you will be just fine. You are a much better person because of who you are. Know it and believe it. If you still are not convinced, spend $10 to $50 for a monthly fee to do a reverse phone check, be verified, or go to websites that can help you verify what you need information on. Even hiring a private investigator would be better than emptying out your bank account. This is so much cheaper than being without money, your savings. National Geographic had a show called *Trafficked with Mariana van Zeller*. The episode titled "Romance Scams" (S2, E2) was suggested by a friend of mine.

So what have I learned in all this that I want to pass along to you?

- ➢ They are just words, and that is all it is.
- ➢ He only cares about your money and wants you to give it to him.

- ➢ You really do not know if you are talking to a man or woman and from what country they are in.
- ➢ When you give away money, can you live without it ever coming back to you?
- ➢ Promises made are just words. Words without action.
- ➢ You cannot make good decisions on feelings or emotions. Use your brain. Use common sense.
- ➢ Any action that needs to be done right now, immediately, is not a good sign, a *red flag.*
- ➢ Do not ignore the *red* flags or your gut feeling. We all have a spirit within us that guides us.
- ➢ It does not matter what he says his status is in life—a military person who knows honor, a hard-working doctor who has gone through schooling, or a successful businessman who is out of the country.
- ➢ Deception is believing a lie. They are just words.
- ➢ Scammers are preying on good people's intentions.
- ➢ They don't care if you go into debt or borrow.
- ➢ Scammers are getting really good at this, really, really good. Do not even start it.
- ➢ God will heal you because He loves you so very much. No doubt about that. He will take the brokenness and make it whole again—just believe.
- ➢ Fear is an emotion.
- ➢ Anything that is not of God, will not prosper. Because all good things come from God.
- ➢ It is prophesied that closer to the end times, more deceit will come.
- ➢ Flattery feeds our pride and is used to get something from you.
- ➢ The first step out of this? DON'T DO IT!

My Prayer for You—from Me to You

Dear Heavenly Father, I thank you for who you are and for your living Word. I pray from the deepest part of my being that You hear my prayer for the one who has read this book. I pray that Your Spirit will come and heal the tears, bleeding, cuts, and bruises on their heart so that they will not hurt anymore. I pray that the evil one that has come to harm be held accountable for their actions. Father, You said in Your Word that the righteous cry out, and the Lord hears and delivers them out of all their troubles (Psalm 34:17). Exodus 14:14 says,

> The Lord will fight for you, and you shall
> hold your peace.

Proverbs 6:31 says,

> Yet if he is caught, he must pay sevenfold,
> though it costs him all the wealth of his house.

I pray that You convict their heart of the deceitful person who has committed the offense against me and others who are reading this book of their wrongdoings and that they see Your glory, Lord. Your Word says this Lord, and I believe it. I plead the blood of Jesus Christ over these words and thank You for all You have given us. I love you, Lord, with all of me. Amen.

The model prayer can be found in 2 Chronicles 20:6–12. This prayer begins with adoration to God, a remembrance of promises, the problem at hand, asking for help, and the thank-you for answered prayers.

Never forget who you are. Never.

About the Author

Joyce Nichols was raised on a farm her whole life. She could drive a tractor before she could drive a truck before she was of age to get a driver's license. Her parents taught her the values of life which included hard work, weekly church services, being honest, paying bills, going to town only when needing something, brushing your hair, and cleaning your face before you leave the house. Other than her brother being someone to play with, her other companion was her imagination. This was the age before cell phones and electronics. Joyce's playground was outside.

Once she was on her own, the next stage of her life was learning that not everyone was raised the same as she was in the country. The world was cruel and telling lies, cheating, stealing, lusting, and having no fear or knowledge or reverence for God was the norm. She felt as though people were alien from her beliefs. Joyce learned that she really did have a good life in the country—a sheltered life with loving parents.

To this very day, Joyce still enjoys life as though she was a kid in an adult body. She wants to see that people are good, somewhere in their souls. Some would say this is looking at the world through *rose-colored* glasses. She supposes this is what makes her books so good and drags you in to read them—her innocence, *rose-colored* glasses, and imagination.

Joyce currently resides in the house she grew up in, flooded with memories of the past and looking forward to new memories and adventures to come and loving God with her whole heart and soul.

If you have found this book to be of help to you or you have questions or comments, please drop a short line to this address, joyce.nichols5734@yahoo.com.